AN
ACLE CHR

ACLE is now pronounced *AYCAL*, although foreigners (those who live north of King's Lynn or south of Lowestoft) often mistakenly call it *ACKLEE*. In the Domesday Book it is spelt ACLE but in 1159 it is recorded as ACHELAI and in 1197 as ACLEE which means that the pronunciation given by foreigners could well be the original one.

The old English spelling is ACLEAH and from this we learn that the name means OAKWOOD, with ley (leah) meaning clearing or open space. Further recordings of OCLE and OAKLEY make this seem a reasonable explanation of the name especially since the Norfolk dialect would account for the change in spelling.

A map of Acle dated 1633 shows a wood to the south of the village and during the Sixteenth century oak trees were cut down and used to build ships for Elizabeth I's navy. Blomefield's Norfolk proposes that the name Acle derives from A-CLEY — a place which is sometimes flooded, as in the case of Cley-next-the-Sea. This alternative explanation has some credibility because the present marshland was part of the sea bed in Roman times, and later became salt marshes and mud flats.

EARLY HISTORY

If we imagine the landscape two thousand years ago at Acle, what is now the the marshland edge was still a beach. Looking south from Acle Church there would have been a stream where now the bypass runs, and at the western edge of the village was a ditch leading north from the river. The valley of the river continued out of Acle past Beighton Church and on to South Burlingham. North of Acle, if you follow the footpath from Piebush Lane to Upton, you can look out across the Bure valley. At Fishley Church the sea may have reached the church itself, with Acle a fishing community situated on the corner of the Bure estuary.

To find the first sign of Stone Age Man in Acle we must rely on discoveries made in recent years. A large stone axe was found near Monies Farm and a polished black flint axe at Damgate Lane. A barbed and tanged arrow head was found in a garden in New Close giving further evidence of Prehistoric Man in the area.

Around 43 AD BC the Romans invaded Britain and ruled until 411 AD. With their organization, culture, and technical expertise they transformed Britain. However, in 61 AD Boadicea, Queen of the Iceni, a tribe which lived in Eastern England, led a revolt against the Roman masters. She herself was killed and her army defeated but her name lives on as a symbol of independence. A gold Icenian coin which forms part of the Evans Collection at the British Museum was found at Acle.

The Roman map of Norfolk shows that two main encampments were located at Caister and at Burgh Castle (Garianonum).

Oddly enough no sign of a fortress has been found at Acle or Tunstall despite their apparent strategic importance. Recently the discovery of a number of coins, a circular stone and a brick construction near Reedham Church gave rise to the hope of finding traces of an outpost near Acle.

In pursuit of this possibility, Peter Dawson of Martham, checked the area of the Bypass with his metal detector in 1987. Between Boat Dyke and the A47 he found Roman pottery fragments and some oyster shells. Later he found a number of Roman coins and a ring all of which he sent to Tony Gregory at the Norfolk Archaeology Unit at Gressenhall for identification.

The ring was a Roman bronze finger ring from the 3rd century. The stone was missing but the adhesive remained. The coins ranged from 98 AD to 270 AD The pottery pieces included various sherds of Roman greyware, two from the third or fourth century of Nene Valley colour coated ware, some Samian Ware, one with part of a maker's stamp on the base, and one of Fourth Century Roman pottery made at Much Hadham, Herts. Other items included two prehistoric struck flints, a Medieval harness pendant from the 13th or 14th century, and the rim of a glazed Grimstone ware jug from the 14th century.

Mr Gregory believes that this was certainly a small Roman site – possibly a farm or one of a group of farm houses.

During the Roman period the great estuary *'Garienis'* began to silt up and by 495 AD a sandbank had appeared. A Saxon Prince named Cerdic and his son Cendrick landed five ships on the bank and named it Cerdic Shore. It is now called Great Yarmouth.

For a while the Saxons dominated the area but in 787 the Danes invaded East Anglia which was extremely important to them . They left a legacy of place names throughout the county – Filby, Ormesby, Stokesby, Hemsby and Clippesby for example – by being the Danish for village. They named the islands to the north of the great estuary East Flegg and West Flegg – flegg meaning flat.

The first Danish settlements were on Fullers Hill in Great Yarmouth which was the only dry land. To the north the inlet known as *"Grubbs Haven"* was silting up and by about 1100 it was completely stopped. Today this area is where the Yarmouth racecourse is located. The channel to the south was near Corton, four miles south of its present position. The marshland was higher than it is today and it is safe to assume that they were salt marshes and that navigation was restricted to what today are river courses.

The dry weather of July 1989 provided perfect conditions to show crop marks from the air and Derek Edwards of the Norfolk Archaeological Unit discovered a unique find in Norfolk. In the Fishley area he photographed an Anglo Saxon settlement with 14 sunkenfloored buildings. These buildings, known as Grübenhauser, were discovered on a sandy outcrop and provide more vital information on the history of this part of Norfolk.

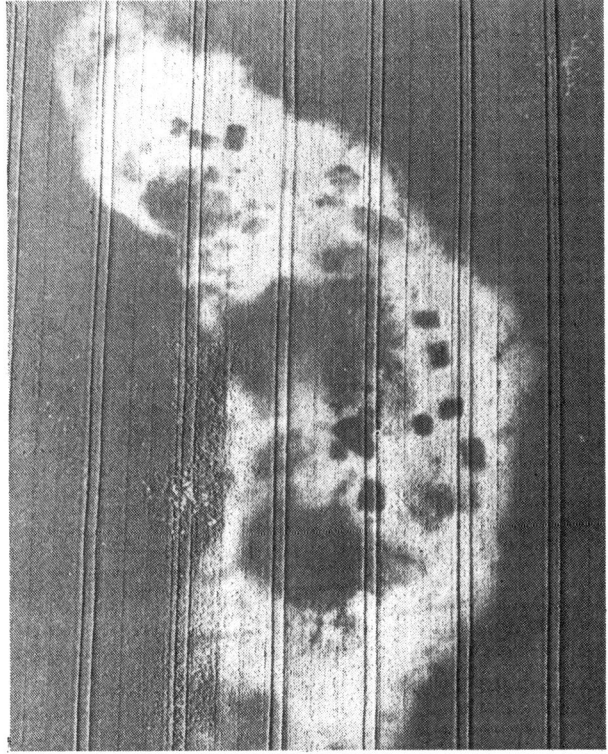

CROP MARKS SHOWING ANGLO SAXON HUT SITES, 30 JUNE 1989. (Photo: Norfolk Archaological Unit, Derek A Edwards.)

THE CONQUEST

One of the most important dates we learn at school is 1066 the date of King Harold's defeat by William the Conqueror at the battle of Hastings. After this famous event an assessment of the conquered lands was carried out and recorded in the Domesday Book.

According to Domesday, Acle had 23 villagers, 38 smallholders and, there had been 3 slaves. There were 15 beehives, 50? acres of meadow, woodland, 40 pigs and one mill.

The village measured one league (about 3 miles) in length and one in width.

We can assume that there was a causeway giving access to the village across the marshes from Billockby and that a ford existed where Acle bridge now stands.

1100 – 1450

Henry I reigned from 1100 to 1135 followed by Stephen of Blois who created Hugh Bigod Earl of Norfolk; with the earldom came the Lordship of Acle. During the early part of the 12th century civil war was rife in England and after Richard I ascended the throne in 1189 the Crusades were a major focus of attention. His brother John's reign saw bloody feuding with the barons and the eventual signing of Magna Carta in 1215.

Henry III became king in the following year. In Acle progress came in the form of dyke digging and the banking up of rivers to stop the flooding of the marshes which were all-important grazing land. In 1253 a charter gave Acle permission for a market – although there had probably been a market in existence long before this date ! In 1272 Yarmouth took the name Magna – Great – and Edward I came to the throne.

During this period Roger Bigot founded Weybridge Priory on a site near Acle bridge and named after Weybrigg the name of the first bridge which had been built in 1101. The Priory for Austen Canons was dedicated to St Mary.

Over the years people have tried to pinpoint the location of the buildings – Priory Close was once believed to be the site but in fact it is the site of the Old Manor House.

A Will left by Ralph Goodwyn in 1518 gave 3s 4d for repairs to the priory at Damesend, Weybridge priory and 6s 8d for repairs to the bridge. The Priory closed in 1536 and the masonry was gradually recycled by the local people. By 1887 only two wagon loads were left. If you take a walk between Calthorpe Cottages and the corner shop in Acle Street you can see a barn containing reused masonry which may have been salvaged from the Priory buildings.

In 1892 builders working for Morgans Brewery found three skeletons near the Bridge Inn — not the first time this had happened. A walk around the area will reward you with some indication of the Priory layout — which may well have been built on an island — and it is hoped that some future arial photography will highlight the features. In the meantime the area has become protected by law and registered as an ancient monument.

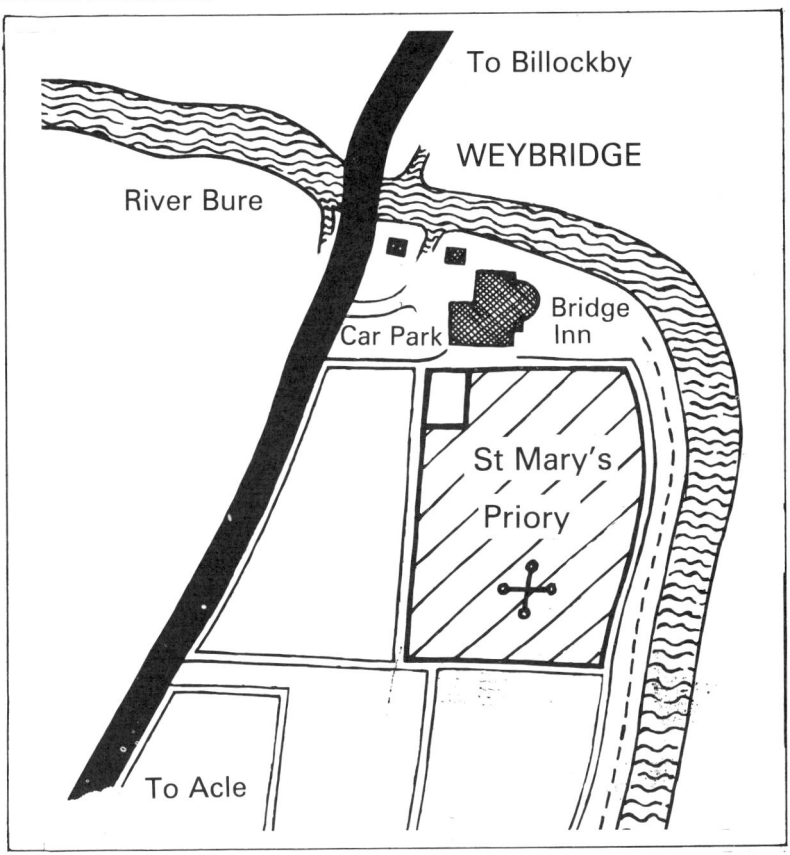

Back to the the 13th Century when the high tides of 1287 flooded the marshes killing Scottish cattle which had been specially imported as a hardy grazing breed. The floods also killed one hundred people in Yarmouth where St. Nicholas Church stood in four feet of water.

The next disaster to strike this part of the world was the Black Death in 1349. It's said that seven of the ten thousand inhabitants of Great Yarmouth perished from the plague.

In 1382 Richard II (1377-1399) granted to the inhabitants of Acle freedom from all tolls and suits of shire and gave them rights of turbary to the Park of Acle. The latter was the right to remove turf, or peat, which was used as fuel.

In 1399 the House of Lancaster began its 62 year reign of England in the person of Henry IV. In the Records Office in Norwich is a Fabric Roll of the Norwich Guildhall dated 1410 – 1411 AD. Part of this Roll names Thomas of Acle in charge of the building of the Guildhall. He became a Freeman of Norwich in 1388 and Sheriff of Norwich in 1415. It is also thought that he may have been the painter of the 'beautiful table' in Norwich Cathedral. This table is probably the re-table now kept in St. Luke's chapel at the Cathedral which was commissioned after the Peasants' Revolt in 1381. The painting on the re-table or reredos depicts the Lord's Scourging, Way to the Cross, Crucifixion, Resurrection and Ascension and is one of the Cathedral's greatest treasures.

ROBERT REYNYS

In the Bodleian Library, Oxford is a book known as *"The Commonplace Book of Robert Reynys of Acle"*. It was translated by the Rev C.L.S. Linnell who has published an account of this fascinating insight into 15th Century life in Acle in a volume of Norfolk Archaeology.

Robert Reynys was born between 1445 and 1450, one of ten children of John Reynys, an Acle carpenter. Robert married Emma in 1471 and they had five sons. After his father's death he followed him as *"churchreve"*.

In the book he tells of *"a gret dredful ffyer in Acle on the 7th of May 1475"*. He also refers to the Charge of the Watch and Constables. In the Charge to the Watch he says:

"if you see or find any fire in a place which be not likely to be quenched without great help ye shall break up their doors and raise the people of this town and do thou pain to quench the fire."

From his book we learn that the battlement of the church steeple was built by John Reynys, John Goodwyn, and Henry Brandon, Churchreves in 1472 and the chancel built by William de Culpho, Rector in 1362.

When the Reverend Linnell translated the book he noted how well thumbed the pages giving weights and measures were, and thought that Reynys may have used the book as a ready reckoner. Part of the book describes the life of St. Ann, a fragment of a mortality play and a long prose account of the life of St Bridget of Sweden. There are also descriptions of Rome, London and various places in the British Isles which give the impression of a well-travelled man, although the Rev Linnell believed that Robert Reynys never went far afield from Acle itself.

Charms for cure of fever, and recipes for the making of ink are preceded by a charm for making an angel appear: This charm states: *"take a child of young age that is between vii and xiii and in the sun set him between your legs and then knit a red silk thread about his right thumb and scrape his nail well and clean and then write these letters A.G.L.A. and then say this prayer:"* (A prayer in Latin then follows after which he goes on) *"And say this prayer with good heart and devoutly and then shall appear iii angels in the child's nails, and let the child say after thee"* (another prayer in Latin).

This strange charm gives us an example of the beliefs and ways of the people in Acle in the 15th Century, but there is no record whether this charm did in fact work. There is one other item in his book which is probably of more interest today than in the times of Robert Reynys and that is the rhymes about birthdays and the signs of the zodiac.

Whoso be born in ye sign of Tauro he schall have moche grace in all best of alle thynges, same in his wyff, same in all he hast.

Whoso be borne in Aries he schall be dredful and shrow grace.

Whoso be borne in Gemini he schall be pore and evyle and have moche desease.

Cancer he schall be pore and evyle of desease.

Leo he schall be bold and a strong theff.

Virgo he schall be wyse and lettyrd.

Libra he schall be schrew.

Scorpio he schall be gret goer in the world.

Sagittarius he schall be hardy and a gret lecher.

Capricorn he schall be riche and loved.

Aquarius he schall be reckless and list for to lose hys men.

Pisces he schall be graceful in all manner.

Robert Reynys probably lived to see the end of the century though the date of his death is unknown and he is last mentioned in a grant dated 1496.

1500 – 1700

The 16th Century is the period of Christopher Columbus and Henry VIII. Religious conflicts were at fever pitch and some of them are illustrated in the life of Bishop Scory who was born in Acle. He appeared before Bonner, the persecuting Papal Bishop and submitted to penance, had formal absolution and became a Papist. He was unhappy in his adopted church, relapsed and went abroad; in 1556 he is reported as Protestant Disputant and the following year made Bishop of Hereford. He was a learned man and credited with translating some of the works of St. Cyprian and St. Augustine. Beside being a turncoat he was accused of enriching himself by moneylending and he died a rich man on 26th June 1585.

One of the most notable events in East Anglian history took place in 1549 – Kett's Rebellion. In August of that year Sir Thomas Cleare and Sir Thomas Woodhouse reached Yarmouth to protect it from Kett's men. To obtain an early warning they dispatched 26 men and provisions for 4 days to Weybridge Priory at Acle.

If you look behind the old Methodist Chapel on Middlesex Lane, you will see a large thatched house which is thought to date from this period.

OLD COTTAGE NEAR ACLE RUN. Part of it is now called Childwall House. This house is probably the oldest in Acle dating from the end of the 15th Century. Inside are oak beams and framework which are now so hard even an electric drill has difficulty penetrating. One door is only four feet high and what is thought to have been a secret passage was found leading from a bedroom to the cellar. The cellar contains niches in the walls and it is believed a tunnel runs from here to the church. The house was once used as the rectory and the grounds stretched from church corner to the railway line and almost to Beighton Road. Carr's plantations, marshes and outbuildings with 2 cottages were within the grounds and the water table was controlled using its own dyke system. A sluice gate and drainage pump existed near the old station Road, going into Acle Run. It was owned by the Calthorpe family until 1860 and land was sold to the Great Eastern Railway to create part of the Railway line.

THE BRIDEWELL

A more notable building of the period is The Bridewell.

The origin of the name comes from London where a house of correction for the idle and vicious was founded in buildings converted from the Royal Palace of Bridewell — built near the site of St Bride's Well between Fleet Street and the Thames.

In 1556 a law was passed to establish houses of correction in its pattern and in 1574 a letter from Sir Francis Walsingham to the Lord Treasurer describes the Bridewell at Acle and refers to it as being recently erected. In that same year Bishop John Parkhurst devised a scheme later to be known as the Acle scheme. It is recorded that he instituted a series of regular meetings at Acle on Wednesdays at monthly or three weekly intervals with Yeomen and Gentlemen. After an hour of prayer, they would discuss the affairs of the Bridewell till lunchtime, after which punishments would be assigned and feuds settled. This system was highly successful and further schemes were introduced in its mould.

Around 1573 a letter by John Parkhurst describes a man called W Ugge – *"A common bull, a vile whoremonger and adulterer, a breaker of mens heddes, a murure, a fethcher of writtes from London, to trouble the poor neighbours, a deliverer of a prisoner out of the stockes at Acle, a companion with promoters, a setter on of promoters to trouble men and get away with their monie, a professed enemie of B. a all (??)godlines a puller of Duitche womens kerches openlie in the market of Gt Yarmouth"*. With such men did the meetings deal.

The Bridewell was eventually divided into cottages and remained so until 1901. The building is still standing today.

In 1588 Sir Francis Drake ended his game of bowls before going to finish off the Spanish Armada. On Saturday 8th October 1597 the Rector of Acle, Mr Thomas Stone, appeared before Bishop Redman to defend a claim by his curate Mr William Robinson that he had more than one benefice, for which he would have to hold a licence. The case was dismissed.

1609 brought high tides and high winds, with the marshland completely under water. An Act known as the Preamble Act of 1609 was passed to try and ensure that the marshland was recovered to its original condition. On the 25th July 1611 Edward Paston wrote a letter to Sir Edmund Paston regarding a piece of marshland at Acle. The marsh known as Stargate Marsh was being claimed to be his by law but Sir William Paston disputed this. The result of this claim is not recorded but it seems the claim arose because of the confusion over marsh names in Clement Paston's Will.

Acle Wood must have been quite extensive at this period – 480 oak trees were cut down in one felling and the people were charged with spoiling the wood. In another instance, James Raunce was charged with having felled 400 oaks, 500 ash trees and 500 loads of wood from Acle woods, and converting the same to his own use, to the Queen's loss. The large house to the North of the village sign dates to this period. It is now called the Manor House but the map of 1633 shows the original Manor House was near the present Post Office. This map is kept at the Norfolk Record Office at Norwich City Library. It was commissioned by Henry Calthorpe, the Lord of the Manor and shows the strip farming system and names the owner of each strip. The larger owners were Burry, Hobart, Palmer and Smithdale. The Boat Dyke was called *"Acle Fleet"* and the allotment land where the link road now runs was called *"Oxcroft"*. The windmill is clearly marked and the road to Norwich passed along Mill Lane and not round the church as it does today. The area now owned by Mr Fred Colk is called *"Churchwaters"* and the present recreation centre area was called *"Nethergate Croft."*

The way from Birlingham Green to Acle Market was a track which goes along the South Walsham Road to the High School and then across the fields to join the farm track which runs behind the High School. This track continues and joins the road now called the windle and at this point a piece of land is called *"Windell Close"* and beside it *"Robin Hoods Dalle"*.

"Bayton Way" is obviously Beighton Road and at the now existing railway bridge is an area called *"Old Mill Hill Furlong"*, while the area south of the railway station is called *"Leffins Croft"*. The Damgate Area was named *"Common called Dangate Heath"* and *"Acle Wood"* was to the east of Moulton Road surrounded by fields known as *"The Groundes of the Lord called the Lawnes"*. In 1653 a record shows that William Burry sold 365 acres and *"The Whitehouse"* to James Calthorpe.

In 1972 when work was being carried out on *"The Whitehouse"*, a 16th century house in the Street, a beam in the roof was found to have a hollowed compartment which may have been used for contraband.

If we move next door to the *"Manor House"*, on the corner of the *"Yarmouth Old Road"* in the Street, it is late 17th Century with 18th century alterations. This house has a remarkable brick vaulted cellar — cruciform — with an oven from which a vent rises to the main fireplace. The house won a restoration award in 1981 and the owner, Mr Field, and the builder Mr Malcolm Porter received the award.

The restoration of this house is exceptional; one of the original windows is intact inside the house, almost all the beams and door frames are exposed and you can see bullocks hair mixed with the plaster in the kitchen. Many of the beams have been drilled with holes and wooden dowels inserted in them, a basic technique of timber-framed building. Some of the beams show where they were chipped away to allow plaster to clinging to them and one decayed beam is left to show what damage Death Watch Beetle can do.

Calthorpe Cottages are also recorded as being built in the 17th Century and have recently been restored.

The causeway to Weybridge is recorded at this time as being in much decay and £400 was required for repairs. The ancient stock is also mentioned as not being employed or profitable as it ought to have been.

In 1634 Bridget Sporle from the Acle Bridewell was hired by a Butcher and found to be vagrant in Norwich. She was punished and sent back to Aylsham where she said she was born.

Before he travelled to Rotterdam in 1639 to see an uncle, Henry Downing, a 33 year old husbandman, took the Oath of Allegiance to the King. This oath was to adhere him to a proclamation made by Charles I in 1635. Downing agreed to return within a month of sailing from the port of Great Yarmouth. The oath was a method of maintaining security - individuals could not hold allegiance to more than one sovereign.

Two fires in Acle were thought to be started by persons of malicious intent, after which the Norfolk Quarter Sessions of October 1650 ordered that a strict watch was to be kept to prevent further incidents.

The 17th Century was a time of turmoil and disaster - the Great Plague in London in 1665, followed by the Great Fire in the following year. Before and after the Civil War (1642-51) witchcraft was a major social and psycological phenomenon and was often used as an excuse for crime. If crops failed, or if animals died, it was easy to blame witchcraft. Marshland and marsh mists seem to figure a great deal in the reports of witchcraft so one may assume that Acle had its fair share and certainly in Great Yarmouth in 1645 sixteen women were tried and five found guilty and hanged.

1700-1800

In 1714 George I of Hanover ascended the throne and in 1721 Robert Walpole became the first Prime Minister. In the same year an act was passed allocating money for the cleansing and deepening of Breydon Water.

A parchment document owned by Mr Michael Field talks of an indenture from John Poynter and his wife to John Knights regarding land in Acle. It is dated 1740 and says that one peppercorn must be paid on the feast day of St. Michael. It also mentions that the turbary is in an area called *"The Doles"* and we know by looking at the 1633 map that the Dole grounds lie between Damgate and Moulton on the edge of the marshes.

Possibly this is the same land previously called Acle Park.

Another item of interest is to do with swans - *"all that liberty of swanning and ancient swan marking"* and that the squire's mark was of a carpenter's square on the bill or beak.

John Poynter crops up again in the Bastardy deeds of 1738 when Lydia Wiley of Acle charges John Poynter of Tombland, Norwich with being the father of her newly born son.

A newspaper advertisement of July 1753 read:

"This is to give notice to all gentlemen, that Monday 23rd of July will be a Bull Baiting at Acle, in Norfolk, and all persons that bring with them good bulldogs shall be maintained gratis. From gentlemen, your humble servants to command John Short of the Queen's Head, Benjamen Howard of the Blue Bell, Thomas Stugell of the King's Head."

The *"Blue Bell"* is now the Ivy covered house house in the centre of Acle and it wasn't until 1835 that Bull Baiting was made illegal.

The draining of the marshes continued but now mechanical means were used. The tower windpumps that can be seen today were probably built on the site of 18th century smock mills.

At Great Yarmouth in 1763 two sailors each received four lashes under each public house sign for stealing merchandise. Poor harvests in successive years — 1765-6 — resulted in a dramatic rise in food prices. There was much local suffering and violent riots were reported in Norwich.

In April 1779, the Bridewell prison was reported as quite out of repair with no water acceptable to prisoners and no straw, no prisoners, and the Keeper's salary at £16.

Nine years later in 1788, a workhouse was built which reached its peak of usage during the extremely hard winter of 1814. It was built on what we now call the New Road but was destroyed by fire in 1834.

A map of Norfolk prepared by William Faden, geographer to George III, and published in 1797 shows the road to Norwich running round the church, and a Toll Gate on the Moulton Road over looking Acle Wood. Damgate is marked as Dangate Heath. A large number of windmills and windpumps are marked on the marshes and there's a windmill to the west of the village. The marshes to the west of the causeway leading to Acle Bridge (shown as Weybridge) are called Fishley Fenn and the public house at the bridge is named the Angel Ale House. Two windmills are visible between Upton and South Walsham and both Stokesby and Reedham Ferries are in existence. The Queen's Head is shown but an interesting anomaly occurs when you look for the Hermitage Inn.

ACLE AS SHOWN ON FADEN'S MAP OF NORFOLK, PUBLISHED IN 1797

The map places the Hermitage near Boat Dyke and the Old Hermitage, which has been called the Rebus since 1986, was then the Ship.

So was the original Hermitage near Boat Dyke and when it closed was the name given to the Ship? Or was it a mistake by the cartographer?

By the end of the century the French Revolution and Napoleon Bonaparte were taking centre stage.

1800 – 1900

In 1805 Norfolk's most famous hero, Horatio Nelson, won the Battle of Trafalgar. In 1807 the slave trade was abolished throughout the British Empire. In 1808 the population of Acle was reported to be 600.

Rapidly thawing snows in the winter of 1809 caused flooding of the marshes. Sailing barges between Norwich and Yarmouth returned home because they could not define the river channel.

Moles were a problem in 1818-Mr Robert Waters of Freethrope was paid £16 for the first year and £8.10 for the next seven years in a contract to keep down the population of the little gentlemen in velvet waistcoats.

By 1821, the population of Acle had increased to 698 and the village was a thriving market community. In 1828 Isaac Lenny a surveyor from Norwich displayed his plan for a new turnpike road for Acle to Great Yarmouth. This road would make the journey to Great Yarmouth shorter by 3 miles 5 furlongs. The previous route is the current road to Caister.

The road was completed by the Acle Turnpike Trust in 1831 and included a new 'Link Road' to join up with the village of Halvergate. It was a great feat of contemporary engineering to build across the boggy marshland and was a major contribution to the development of Acle.

Tollgates were erected along the road, one in Great Yarmouth, one on Wooden Hut Corner at Halvergate and the Acle Toll Gate was approximately 600 yards west of Tunstall Boat Dyke Bridge on the Acle Parish Boundary.

Coaches from Norwich to Yarmouth were soon running 4 times daily and the Royal Mail was in competition with the Dart. A new bridge was built on the old route to Yarmouth; it had three arches and lasted until 1931 when the present bridge was built.

The Tithe map of the 1830s shows a brick kiln to the east of Acle Health Centre and Pyebush Lane is called Nethergate Lane. Acle Decoy Broad is shown on the marshes and the land from Mill Lane to the church is called Sand Pit Piece.

Queen Victoria was crowned in 1837 and by 1841 the population of Acle had risen dramatically to 860. In August 18 1848 the Yarmouth Independent published the village news and included an article on the Acle Flower Show.

It quotes Mr H Back, Chairman of the organization which arranged the event, as saying that one hundred and fifty carts, gigs and carriages attended together with up to six thousand people. It also reports an argument between Mr Back and the vicar. It seems that Mr Back arranged a site for the pig pens to be fixed and the Rector ordered them to be removed. The gossips of the village were saying that the Rector would not allow the Rectory grounds to be used again, so all were reminded of the damage that gossip can cause by an appropriate piece of poetry:-

Oh! could there in this world be found
Some little spot of happy ground
Where village pleasures might go round
Without the village tattling.

How doubly blest that place would be,
Where all might dwell in liberty,
Free from the bitter misery
Of gossip's endless prattling.

If such a spot were really known Dame peace
might claim it as her own,
And in it she might fix her throne,
For ever and for ever.   *(9 more verses)*

Around 1850 Goddard Johnson wrote a small history of Acle which is now kept in the Norfolk Record Office. It includes a copy of a grant by Roger Bigot (of the three Rogers — 1177, 1225, 1305 — which one is not clear) — but it does refer to the park supporting timber and of him having a mansion in Acle. Goddard Johnson also refers to a grant of 1496 which mentions Robert Reynes (sic) and is witnessed by Master Philip Beynham, Rector of Acle, Henry Everard, William Gay, John Frye and many others.

Joseph Jay was the surgeon in Acle in 1858 and he bought Ivy House where he practised until his death in 1871. William Cufaude together with his son Frank paid Mrs. Jay £150 for the goodwill of the practice in 1871.

In 1859 a grant was made for a school together with land (1 rood, 23 perches) to provide a school house and yard bounded on the west by the Norwich and Acle Turnpike. The grant was made to the Rector and Churchwardens and is signed by the Rt. Hon. Frederick Lord Calthorpe and the Hon. Frederick Henry William Gough Calthorpe.

1878 was the severest winter for many years: flooding in November, then the marshes covered with ice for several weeks and the bad weather continued for seven months. The Parish Room was erected in Acle in 1880 at a cost of £300 and a Primitive Methodist Chapel built in 1883.

In 1888 the Yarmouth Independent reported the arrest in Great Yarmouth of Mr George Scott charged with being a wandering lunatic. An article next to this in the paper told of a concert held in the Parish Rooms at Acle with Mr Capon at the piano and a chorus of some 40 children. The village of Fishley by then contained only twelve residents all of whom were reported as being very poor.

The Norwich to Great Yarmouth railway had been opened in 1844 and on the 12th March 1883 the Great Eastern Railway opened the line between Great Yarmouth and Acle. This line was continued to Brundall which was of great importance in the development of Acle.

By 1891 Acle had a population of 933 and cattle sales were held every Thursday. White's Directory of 1896 listed Mr A Squire as Fire Brigade Superintendent with one manual fire engine. There were numerous tradesmen in the village including saddlers, a wheelwright, a watch repairer, a shoe maker, sexton, steam miller, stone mason, and insurance agent. There was a branch of Barclay's bank, the school showed an average attendance of 150 and the Police Station had one Sergeant, twelve Constables and a Superintendent named Charles Parr.

The last wherry travelled down Tunstall Dyke to Tunstall Staithe in 1897. Named *"The Albert and Alexandra"*, the wherry was owned by Joseph Powley, a coal merchant. For the wherry to pass under the Acle Straight the water had to be just the right level. The wherry plug would be removed to let in water to lower the craft when it was light. The *"Albert and Alexandra"* was an 18 ton wherry and the *"Atlanta"* owned by Porter of Acle was a 24-ton wherry whose last skipper was Bob Harris at the end of the 19th Century.

Acle had two chapels at this period-one Wesleyan and the other Primitive Methodist.

On 4th December 1897 Norfolk News published an article headlined *"A Talk with an Acle Patriarch"*. It provides a wonderful review of the 19th Century so I shall quote it in full:

WHEN THE CENTURY WAS YOUNG

A TALK WITH AN ACLE PATRIARCH

MEMORIES OF NELSON'S FUNERAL

BACK TO THE DAYS OF BONEY

It is not given to every man to sow his own 'taters at the age of ninety-six.' Edmund Harrison of Acle will be ninety-seven next April and he has performed that very service this very year. It goes without saying that 'tater sowin' could be better done by a younger man. Indeed, if his widowed daughter, who lives with him, had her venerable parent under perfect control she would command him "to keep quiet" and rest in his chimney corner. "he du stick his feet in the flower beds so, father du, when he works in the garden". But father is not conscious of these shortcomings. A man with a son of 74 and a daughter of 78 might excusably regard himself as a spent force.

Not so the patriarch of Acle. To all and sundry he opposes the spirit of a man who would still be a factor in the world's affairs. His daughter-companion would seem to be a mere chit of a thing to judge from the way he deals with her when she traverses his views. So he potters in and out his garden as the whim inclines. All Norfolk might be ransacked to find a pleasanter retreat, of its kind, for ruminative age. Fronting the thatched and white-washed cottage there are a few box-lined flower beds. Further on is a patch or two devoted to the cult of the cabbage. From every point there is a sweeping view of the breezy flats that lie between Acle and the sea. Yarmouth, with its towers and chimneys, lies darkly fringed against the horizon. The interior of the cottage is typical of peasant life in Norfolk-a brick floor; a low-pitched roof; in the window a few pot plants; on the walls some pious prints with German titles and brown varnished frames; on the mantel-shelf some faded photographs, and here and there some simple texts "that teach the rustic moralist to die".

• •

OLD POTTLES

Ensconced in his wonted corner, with his feet to a big fire, Harrison can talk with the measured pertinacity of an eight-day clock. His hearing seems to be perfect. He has a strong full-fleshed, dignified face. A fringe of white hair straggles out from under the rim of a soft sombrero. Sometimes, when a memory of more than usual vividness occurs to him, his eye lights up, and he gesticulates with his stick like a field marshal in the presence of the enemy. He did so when he asked me if I knew Old Pottles.

No I didn't know anyone named Pottles.

"Well, p'raps he was afore your time. Why he died at a hundred and seven, and I ha' known him when he was ninety-five walk from Acle to Ludham. He was a rare ole smuggler, he was. In them days there was a rare lot o' that goin' on in these here parts; but o' course there worn't such a look out as there is now.

I remember once a rare lot o' stuff was landed on Caister beach. It was put on a wagon; but a feller on hoss-back catched 'em up and told em the orficers were arter 'em up and so what du they du but hull the whole cargo in Burlingham Pit, and the orficers never found it nayther. I was never in the smugglin' line werry much myself, but I might ha' bin. One mornin' when I was about twenty-five I had to go an' see a man what lived at Neatishead. He kem down afore he was properly dressed, and he drew out o' a shud an ole' tin pot full o' gin.

'Now', says he, du you drink that up'. I said, 'if you gi' me a little water I'll drink some '. But he didn't du that. He drunk a little hisself, and left me the rest. I wouldn' ha' much, cause I knew that wouldn' suit me, bein' as I worn't used to it.

But lor', that was beautiful Hollands gin. He tried all manner o' ways to get me to jine wi' him. 'look here' says he, 'you be up at Acle Bridge at tew o'clock to-morrow mornin', an' there'll be a couple o' tubs o' gin for you.' I kem home and told my wife and she said, 'If you git them in here I git out here.'

She said she worn' goin' to be stripped bare for a tub o' gin.. So I never went. But the gin was there, and that lay in ole Porter's warehouse for two months. Ah, there was a sight o' smugglin' goin' on at Acle Bridge.

●●●●●●●●●●●●●●●●●●●●●●●●●

WHEAT FOUR POUND A COOMB.

"Why, I can remember when wheat was four pound a coomb."
"Yes, put in the widowed daughter, an' your father kep' a donkey - "Howd your tongue" said Harrison, taking the reins of the story into his own hands. "My father used to set me on the donkey, gi' me a guinea tied up in his pocket hankerchief, and send me to Moulton Mill for a bushel of wheat meal. My father had seven on us at home-how we all lived God A'mighty know-an' he got fourteen pound into miller's debt at Strumpshaw.

"He had six acres o' land, and all his own, my father had. When the harvest was over he troshed three acres o' wheat, an' wi' this he paid his debt off. He made four pound a coomb of his wheat, an' that set the ole man right on his legs agin. I couldn't ha' bin more'n four years old when I rode on top o' the sacks to Strumpshaw Mill. I can remember my poor mother had white herrin' for her supper when I got home, an' my father he threw the money on to the table an' he say 'There, Sairey, bor, we're out o' debt, thank God.'

"I can call to mind right well that when I rode on top o' the corn sacks to Strumpshaw there were flags on the church steeples. What for? Why, they was to be took down if Boney kem. But ole Nelson wouldn't let him come here, ye know. Ah, I can remember Nelson's funeral as if it were yesterday. My mother went up to Norwich and bought a picture. I was only about five years old then.

"And of course you remember the rejoicings after Waterloo?

"There worn't much rejoicing about these parts. People were in the dumps. Corn kem down too quick. But I can remember the fust peace being proclaimed.

There was tables set out from one end o' Acle street to the other. I was apprenticed to a bricklayer then. I remember that the tubs o' beer stood right round the tree in front o' the Queen's Head. I didn't know the beer was free, so I pulled out twopence for a pint, an' the man he say 'put up PEACE AND FREE BEER your money, boy, beer is free to day.' Then, you know, Boney got loose and raised another army.

After these miscellaneous reminiscences, Harrison harked back to the beginning of his history. "I was born at Beighton, and of course I didn't have no larnin'. There was only one school about these parts in them days, and that was at Acle. My fust start in life was to go scare-crowin' at eighteen-pence a week an' my Sunday dinner. Then next I went to live along wi' my uncle at South Burlingham. Ah! that was a terrible hard winter. I think that must have been in 1814. There was a lot o' people frozen to death, an' a good many starved. That was a bad time. The workhouse about here was more'n full. The poor folks could not all be got in. They had to be put in shuds and canvas things, an' I don't know what all. This workhouse was down the New Road an' it was burnt down fifty or sixty year ago. By the way, I was the fust man that ever put a tool into the new road from Acle to Yarmouth. Well I remember that the werry same year as this hard winter there was a rare wet harvest. On Michaelmas Day when we were gettin' our fourses my uncle he says to me says he 'I think we'll ha' some o' that wheat,' for he thought about puttin' it in the barn so that he could get it out for seed. He said to me, 'You take the hosses.' The stable door was right agin the barn door, an' I heard him keep a-sayin' 'Lord ha' mercy on us!' Just then there was a brilliant light, and everything was as bright as ever I see in my life. I bolted, an' on every step I took I felt as if I was a-jammin' on great squares o' glass. I don't know what it was — some kind o' meter thing.

· "Anyhow, when I got in the house it was full o' frightened people. Next I went out as a town boy. Town boy? Why, that mean that I got no wages, only my clothes and my grub. After that my father put me to the bricklayin'. O' course I had to sarve the bricklayers fust. My hands got that sore with handlin' the bricks I couldn't rest day nor night.

HIRING SESSIONS

So I ran away to the hirin' sessions at Acle. In them days you could go an' let yourself out at Michaelmas. Ladies used to come up here and hire their maids. I was a agreein' wi' a man about wages, when up come my uncle, and he say-he used to talk gruff, just like ole Billy o'Yarmouth-he says, says he, 'I thought you was a bricklayer ! What d'ye think your father'll say ?' Then he say, 'How are ye on for shoes?' 'Well,' I say, 'I hain't got no more'n what I got on.' 'Well,' he say, 'You go to Evans's an' tell him to make you tew par,' Then we went along o' my uncle an' spent the shillin' for hirin' money. My new master was Mr Moll, an' he gev me seven pound a year as a boy to work on the land an' live in the house. The farm labourers used to live in the house, an' the maid servants an' the men servants too. We an' the missus an' the master all sat in one room, though they had a table to theirselves. I bein' the boy had to lay along wi' the head man. One night I heard the geese flutterin' about. 'Lay still, boy,' he say 'You're allus heerin' suffin." At last he heard 'em hisself, an' he say 'You're right, boy, there's someone arter them geese.' He upped the winder, an' there was a feller wi' one in one hand an' one in t'other. 'Leave us one for our Christmas dinner' the man wi' me called out. 'We ha' left you tew,' the other feller say! An' so he had. At least twenty must ha' been stole. We never used to hev any beef except at Michaelmas time. All the rest o' the year we had pork. We used to kill a pig about once a fortnight. Many a time I ha' seen the farmers' wives go to market on hossback wi' tew great baskets, one on one side on 'em and one on t'other. We didn't grow many mangel in them days, an' yet swedes. They were all white tarnips. Arter this I went and helped plant some trees at Thorpe. Next I got work in a saw pit an' I used to earn sometimes three pound a week; but the foreman robbed the master and then the pit was shut up. What to do I didn't know. At last I an' another man hired a foot machine."

A PRIMITIVE TROSHIN' MACHINE

Foot machine? Why that's a thing what you go troshin' with. That's like jammin' upstairs, an that took nine men to work it. You work yourself on an' you work yourself off, and then you go shuggin' the straw till that's your turn to go agin. But arter a time we could not git the fellers to stick to it, and that was too hard to work ourselves. At one place, Hellesdon, we got a lot o' soldiers out o' barracks to come an' lend us a hand. Next I got a job at Catton Hall; but one of the servants played the rogue wi' the clock so that it wouldn't go, and I got turned off wi' the rest. After this I kem home to my own parish an' I worked for a farmer at a shillin a day. Corn was werry cheap then. I asked him to hain my wages, an' he said he could get plenty o' men to work for him for my price. He was a nasty hungrifyin feller. Next I went as ostler, to look arter the coach hosses. Five coaches used to run through here every day the. I had always eight hosses in the stable. Soon Hogarth and Durrant's coaches came up, and Sword's got run off the road. So here I was, out agin. At last I got made sick bagman to Mr Hogarth at Yarmouth. Sick bagman? Oh,! that man. I had to look arter the sick hosses. The work was so hard I hadn't time to get my wittles. One day I went to Acle Fair wi' a lot o' the other fellers, and we all got so drunk Mr Hogarth paid us off in a hurry. Next I went on the land agin. Then I went into the hay-trade, an' I used to take hay to Norwich an' Yarmouth, but I couldn't get on at Yarmouth, 'cause the money wasn't good. They used to promise to pay ye when the fishin' was over. But the fishin' never was over. I liked Norwich best 'cause as soon as you uncarted, there was the money."

At this point Harrison began to show just a trace of weariness. he went on with his story, however, describing how he came to take Acle King's Head, how he had outlived three wives, and so forth.

"Now will ye hev a nice glass of home-brewed beer? Now du."

I left him standing in his doorway shading his eyes from the pallid November sun beams, and pointing to a bush of red rose growing up the lintel and still in full bloom.

Alas on the 27th January 1898 Mr Edmund Harrison's death appeared in the newspaper. He died at his home in Damgate at the age of 97. It seems that a neighbour Mr Munford, fell down and died in Mr Harrison's house, no doubt the shock of this brought on his own death.

NOWHERE

Under the provision of the Assessment Act of 1862 *"Nowhere"* was annexed to the parish of Acle. The location has been something of a mystery; some people located it on the boundary between Fishley and Acle while others believed it to be on the marshes near Damgate. I can say after much research that it was none of these.

The story seems to go back to the 11th Century when many villages had salt pans, which were salt marshes flooded by high tides. They were dammed off and the sun dried the marsh leaving a residue of salt. The salt was collected and used for the preservation of fish and food stuffs. The surrounding parishes therefore had isolated marshes miles from their boundaries, some as saltings, and today these extra-parochial marshes continue to be part of these parishes. Halvergate is recorded in the Domesday Book as having a salt pan but I can find no record of one at Acle, but some of the parish marshes are miles from ANYWHERE: NOWHERE in fact.

In the 1940s the Norfolk Archaeological Unit excavated a site which contained a mound of earth behind Ash Tree Farm and found Medieval pottery and Ash. Tony Gregory believes that this was the site of the salt pans. This area is annexed to Acle parish and is about a mile from Yarmouth beside the Bure to the north of the Acle Straight. This land is part of *"Nowhere"* but the name changed in the early part of the Twentieth Century to White House Farm.

It was the Bailey family who altered the name after Mr Bailey had a 'run in' with the law. The story goes that Mr Bailey went to Great Yarmouth to sell some cattle and after a successful day, decided to celebrate his good fortune. The Yarmouth Constabulary had reason to speak to him and asked his place of residence. His reply of *"Nowhere"* did not convince the policeman and put him in deeper trouble. I cannot relate the conclusion of this story except that he was advised to change his address which he did shortly afterwards to White House Farm.

There is no doubt about the area being annexed to Acle because a 19th Century Map in the Norfolk Record Office shows the extra parochial marshes as part of an area called Nowhere. So the next time you drive down the Acle Straight you can look out towards Caister and say- *"There is Nowhere"* !

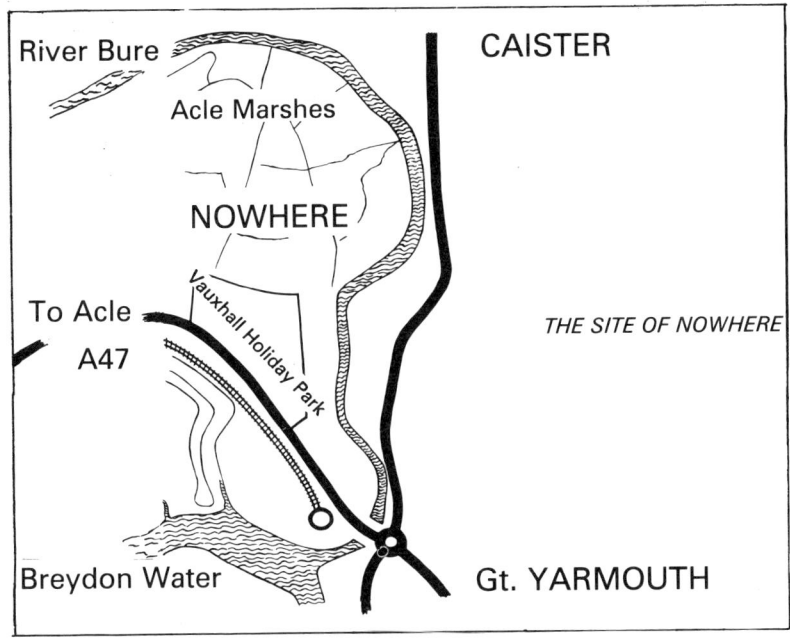

ACLE WINDMILL

The Domesday Book mentions a mill in Acle but this was without doubt a Water Mill the location of which is unknown. However the 1633 map shows a windmill to the west of the village which was a "Post Mill". The mill was advertised for sale in 1768 as a "Double Windmill" with 4 acres of freehold land nearby. It was sold again in 1821 by auction at the Queen's Head Inn and was said to have been lately rebuilt. It had a large roundhouse, two pairs of french stones, and a flour mill. There is no more mention of the "Post Mill" but a "Tower Mill" was built on the site in 1836 and in November of that year the cap was blown off in a storm. In 1838 the Tithe Award names Samuel Bell as the owner and Robert Ward as the occupier.

The mill was auctioned in 1845 when it was described as a new brick-built tower windmill with seven floors, patent sails driving three pairs of stones, with flour mill, jumper and requisite going gears.

By 1858 the mill was being worked by James Faulke and five years later was let to John, William and Albert Squire. In 1889 it was up for auction again — this time as a steam and brick tower mill. It had the addition of bakery with a recently built oven, a cucumber house next to the boiler house, and machinery consisting of a Holmes 18 horse power vertical steam engine with boiler and shafting to drive three pairs of stones in the steam mill, or three pairs of stones in the windmill with belting.

ACLE WINDMILL

It was not sold successfully until 1893 when George Disney of Burgh Castle bought it for £340. In the great gale of 1895 the tower was damaged and wreckage strewn 40 yards away. Worse was to come.

A severe storm in October 1904 broke over Norwich and district. Mr Disney thought to take advantage of the winds and went at daybreak on the 8th to start the mill. However, the winds were so strong that the sudden action of starting the machinery caused the worm governing the fly and sails to break. This was immediately followed by the breaking of the shafting between the sails and the cogs. The force of the wind took full hold of the sails caused the whole of the head of the mill to lurch forward into the face of the wind and it was held there by pressure.

The mill was sold by auction in 1907 for £250 to Mr S J Tallowin. It was never to work again and eventually disappeared from the landcape.

SMITHDALE'S FOUNDRY

The Smithdale family owned a foundry in Norwich in the middle of the 19th century and produced the original machinery for mustard-making on behalf of the Colmans. It seems that Smithdales realised the potential sales of mustard and started producing their own *"Smithdales Mustard"*. Not surprisingly perhaps, they lost their contract for machinery from the Colmans. So they decided to move their foundry to Panxworth where the railway was planned. When the railway was re-routed to Acle instead, they bought a slaughter house there and opened a new foundry near the Bridewell in 1892. The foundry included a forge, a pattern shop and a workshop. The furnace was a Copola Furnace made at the works with a steam engine for the blast.

The name of Smithdale became famous for marsh drainage because they built the last windpump in Norfolk at Ash Tree Farm and Thomas Smithdale invented a pump which for many years was the standard one for marsh drainage. The company won a silver medal for their work and expanded rapidly, employing 87 people in its hey day.

There are many stories told by Mr Dudley Blake of Acle who worked for Smithdales for most of his life. As a lad he used to sit on top of a windpump as a lookout while the workers went fishing. He tells of being called to Catfield during the Second World War. A plane had crashed into a marsh pump hut scattering it all over the marsh and he had to remove the plane's propeller from the dyke. He was brought to tears when he found the pilot's head in the nearby trees and for many years he used the pilot's helmet when riding his motor bike.

Mr Arthur Smithdale was responsible for inventing a gas maker and it was advertised as the simplest on the market. In 1908 it was reported as running trouble-free for 8 months at Acle and the burner gave 75 candle power at a penny for twenty hours.

By the 1920s the family held an influential position in the village and their business moved with the times. They made steam engines, oil engines, and eventually installed electric pumps to drain the marshes.

After the Second World War business gradually declined and in 1974 the foundry was closed and the contents sold at a giant auction. Fortunately, Gressenhall Rural Life Museum purchased a substantial amount of the machinery where it can be seen today.

ACLE FIRE SERVICE

As I have already mentioned organized fire watches began at least as early as the 15th Century. For more up-to-date information I consulted

John High who served the local Fire Brigade for 33 years and is a well loved character in the village. He decided to write a short history of the Fire Brigade from which I have drawn the following account.

The first horse-drawn fire engine was stationed in a brick shed on Damgate Lane near the home of the superintendent, Mr Furrance. In the early part of this century it was moved to another shed near the old Primary School. It was a Merryweather Hand Pump with twelve handles on each side for pumping.

When a fire call was received the local policeman would mount his bicycle and go round the village informing the voluntary firemen that they were needed. If it was dark he would throw pebbles at the appropriate windows. During the winter the two horses were kept at Mill Lane but in summer they were kept on the marshes which could could create problems. Mr Dawson, now aged 88, remembers going to collect the horses from the marsh on one occasion and finding one horse in a dyke and the others nowhere to be found. No horse meant no fire engine, so the fire had to take its course. As John High says, those were the good old days as long as it wasn't your house on fire!

A regular conversation on the way to the fire in those days went:

"Can you see a glow in the sky yet George?"
"No, not yet, Fred."
"Then slow them bloody horses up so we can earn a bit more cash when we get there."

It was normal at this time to have four members to ride on the engine and recruit men at the fire. The recruits would receive 10 old pence per hour. The problem was that at the start the water came out at full bore but as time passed, the men tired and the jet dwindled away to a trickle.

Around the 1920s Mr Ashby Coleman removed the shafts from the engine and fitted a draw bar so it could be towed by a Model T Ford. The first fire after this conversion, the two were connected together but with the pin upside down. It wasn't long before they parted company although the damage was slight.

In 1928 Halvergate School caught fire and the Acle engine was called. On arriving they found the nearest water supply was the village pond about 200 yards away which the crew thought was too far for the hose. The Superintendent settled the argument; he measured from the fire to the pond with a 2ft rule and found they had just enough hose. By now, of course, the school was gutted but the house next door was saved although it had taken 26 men pumping to create a full jet.

In 1939 a permanent fire station was built and during the Second World War it became part of the National Fire Service and afterwards the

Norfolk Fire Service. John High joined this service in 1952.

Most call outs in this period were for stack fires and reed beds set alight by passing steam trains. It was common to be called out across the river Yare. The fire engine had to cross Reedham Ferry but the 400 gallons of water on board was too heavy so it had to be let out on the way and the tanks refilled from the river.

When Hassingham Church caught fire, John worked inside passing out furnishings and plate to the door. There was a loud crash above him and the roof came tumbling down. *"I closed my eyes and thought: 'This is it',"* he says. *"Something brushed both my arms and when the dust settled, I opened my eyes to see two massive roof beams laid each side of me."*

Later that day John was hosing down the inside walls of the church aware of the colour wash peeling off. As it washed away a text in gold and green was revealed: *"Honour thy Mother and thy Father and your days on earth will be long."* From that day on John thought someone was watching over him.

Today the Acle Fire Brigade has moved into the age of technology and the station is manned by eleven retained firemen. There are about 180 call outs a year ranging from cows in dykes to chimney fires. In 1988 the station received a new engine with electronically controlled pumps and a high pressure pump. The firemen have electronic bleepers-the days of pebbles at windows are over.

ST. EDMUND'S CHURCH

Many churches are built on sites of Martyr's shrines and possibly Acle church is one of those. There is no mention of it in the Domesday Book but some people believe that it dates to the end of the 11th Century. Because of its round tower there is a misconception that it is Saxon but recent research has proved that this is not conclusive. Round-towered churches were built after the Saxon period.

There are suggestions that the Acle Church tower is built on old footings of a defensive tower and that a fire destroyed the church which was then rebuilt in the 13th Century, but there is no proof for this hypothesis.

What we do know is that in 1221 Henry III presented Ralph de Norwich to this church and the names of the Rectors appear from then on. The building is therefore the oldest left in the village and is of great importance to Christians and non-Christians alike.

Before entering the church by the south porch there are two items of interest. To the side of the porch on the left is an old coffin of Purbeck marble of origin unknown. To the left of the outside door is a stone wall marked as a sundial although the metal pointer has now broken off. It was supposed to show the time of the four masses but this dial shows five-the fifth being the mass for sailors, a reminder of the times when Acle was a port.

The church is entered by a large oak door. In the Vestry are some deeds dated 1551 and 1548 regarding the Market Place in Acle, and a chalice dated 1837. Two other chalices have been removed and kept elsewhere.

The Font dates back to 1410 but the cover is a 1934 replica of one at Castle Acre. The panels show the four evangelists, a Pieta, God's love in sacrifice, the Blessed Trinity and the instruments of the Passion. At one time it would have been richly painted and gold-leafed. The brass plaque on the Font mentions the Minstrels' Gallery which is above the South Porch entrance. It was constructed in 1934 and was made from timber from the school some of which came from the school desks.

The Bell Tower is a *"free-standing"* with only one other like it in the country. If the tower fell down the six bells would stay up. The bells are a 10cwt Tenor, three dated 1623, one dated 1654, and the Treble dated 1933. In 1946 the original second and third bells were re-cast by Gillett and Johnston who also made the Treble.

During excavations for the Bell Tower in 1933, ashes and molten lead were found in the base of the tower which gave rise to speculations about a fire in the early medieval period and the church lying in ruins until the 13th Century when the present Nave was built. The top of the Tower has an octagonal area which Robert Reynys mentions in his book and cost £16 in 1472. The statues on the top represent the four evangelists with two Kings and two Bishops, and looking southeast towards his palace at Reedham is St. Edmund, with St. Humbert who was martyred with him. The respective arms of St. Edmund and the See of Norwich are emblazoned on the shields below.

On the string course there is the figure of a monk looking towards St. Mary's Priory at Weybridge. Looking towards the Chancel you can see the 15th Century Rood Screen which was restored in 1914. There is a belief that this screen did not originate in this church and might have been brought from St. Mary's Priory but there is no proof.

The original Rood Screen for the church must have stretched the complete width of the Nave and the original staircase was from an outside door on the north side.

The staircase to the Roodloft was probably moved to the south side and the newel staircase built in order to make room for a fifth altar.

Inside the remains of the staircase above the entrance is a painting in red ochre of what looks like a face breathing fire. It is thought to be all that is left of a larger painting and this part represents a dragon. Another painting near the pulpit reported in 1894 was supposed to show two soldiers in uniform circa 1370 but no trace of this can now be found.

At one time there would have been a walkway or gantry above the Rood Screen and hanging above this would have been a crucifix as there is today. At the time of the Reformation, when the King became head of the Church, the crucifix was removed and the royal coat of arms put in its place. The royal coat of arms hanging near the stairs dates from William IV.

At the bottom of the staircase is an archway which was discovered in 1929 and around which there is great controversy. In 1931 the Rev Williams applied to Norwich Consistory Court to have it erected in the church although it was opposed by many in the village. It is said that the stones forming the archway were removed from *"puddock holes"* — holes made for scaffold which were in the Nave and which were part of a Norman doorway. This doorway was believed to be the old door to the Nave but when the present Nave was built in the 13th Century the floor was raised by two feet. The doorway was of no use, being too low, and was taken down and the stones used to fill the scaffold holes.

The Court agreed that the removal of these stones was most improper but even more damage could be done if they were put back and eventually it was erected where you see it today.

Before moving to the Chancel, take a look at the roof of the Nave made of pine and constructed about 1907. There is of course another roof over this one and it possible to walk between the two as long as you don't mind the spiders.

The Chancel was built in 1362 by William de Culpho, Rector of Acle. As you walk up to the altar the vivid colouring of the stained glass window becomes apparent. The window which is typically Victorian was constructed in 1867. Under the north east window of the Chancel is a brass dated 1627 and on the same side towards the nave is an inscription now protected by a cover.

This inscription was only discovered in 1912 and is remarkable not only for surviving but also because it was written in charcoal on the original plaster wall. Many scholars have inspected it and the conclusion was that it was written before the Black Death in 1349. However, we now know that this is impossible because the chancel wasn't built until 1362. C.G. Coulton M.A. published an article in Volume 20 of Norfolk Archaeology which argued for a date in the 15th Century. The mention of horned hats, which were not in use until the early 1400s, and the handwriting point to a date before 1471. There were many plagues around this time-1406 and 1449 seem to be the favourites. A rough translation of the inscription is as follows:

"*O lamentable death-how many dost thou cast into the pit:
Anon the infants fade away, and the aged, death makes an end.
Now these, now those, thou ravishest, O death on every side.
These that wear horn (headress) or veils fate spareth not.
Therefore while in the world the brute beast Plague rages hour by hour.
With prayer and with remembrance deplore deaths deadliness.*"

Whoever the author and whenever it was written, it provides a look back into our history and paints a horrifying picture.

Walking back to the Font, to the left of the south porch is a list of the Ten Commandments. A slab north of the Font is inscrcibed to Edward of the ancient house of Wynn who died in 1652. The Wynns of the House of Gwyder were of the first rank in Cambrian genealogy and descendants of the Kings of Wales dating back to Celtic days. They are now extinct. How he came to be buried in Acle is not known but he must have been in poor circumstances because the inscription is on a slab of an earlier monument. The coat of arms, although damaged seems quite correct, however.

The North Porch of the Church was built under the bequest of Robert Bataly of Acle in 1494. On the sill of the East Window is written "*GOD SAVE THE KINGE 1616*" which was probably occasioned by the King James I Authorized version of the Bible.

This is but a small piece of the history of Acle Church. If you visit it I can only ask you to contribute a donation to the maintenance of this wonderful building and its antiquities.

The Church decorated for Christmas during the 19th Century.

Exterior looking west.

PHOTOGRAPHS OF ACLE

MR ROBERT BAKER'S FARM 1863

A FOWLER PLOUGHING ENGINE AT ACLE

ACLE NEW ROAD DURING THE FLOOD OF 1878

THE ACLE AUCTION MART 1878.
The auction was held on Mill Lane. Centre right is the rear of the old Queen's Head and the top of Ivy House can be seen centre left.

ACLE BRIDGE circa 1880. To the left is a load of Limestone brought by wherry and then taken by wheelbarrow to the lime kiln. The publican and owner of the lime kiln was Benjamin Porter whom Edmund Harrison referred to as a smuggler.

ACLE BOAT DYKE. Probably taken during the flood of 1878. In the background is the public house "The Hermitage". It was on the causeway to Weybridge Priory and a likely site for an old hermitage attached to the Priory.

HIGHS FAIR VISITING ACLE. Probably 1870-1880 and a major event for the village. Possibly an annual event, the fair continued to visit Acle well into the 20th Century but on a much smaller scale and was later known as Rhubarb's Fair. It was held either on the street or at the Bridge Inn.

THE FLOUR WAGON OUTSIDE THE BAKER'S SHOP ON THE YARMOUTH OLD ROAD. The flour wagon was owned by J J Colman, Carrow, Norwich and made regular deliveries. At first glance it appears that the wagon is being pulled by three horses but on closer inspection the front horse is not a horse at all, but a mule.

SAM WELLS THEATRE AND CIRCUS AT THE OLD BARN ON THE WAY TO NEW ROAD. This photograph was taken around 1870 and is recorded as the barn on the way to New Road used as a theatre 40 years ago. The photograph seems to have been deliberately touched up to create the look as it was in 1830.

THE BLACKSMITHS SHOP. The Blacksmith was Mr John Wilkerson and his assistant was Sidney King. There were 2 forges and 4 horses could be worked at once. A round metal plate was in the rear yard for forming cart wheels. John Reuben Wilkerson became Master Farrier in 1901 and retired in 1931. The building was converted to a drapers shop until it was changed to a hardware shop in recent years. Note the plough in the photograph has a wooden sledge under the blade so as not to damage the road. The anvils and equipment are now at Gressenhall Rural Life Museum. The celebrated artist Mr Owen Waters was born in this house and he still lives in Acle today.

A GIPSY PARTY ALONG PYEBUSH LANE. They do look rather well dressed for gipsies but if you look closely at their faces and particularly their noses there is a family likeness. The lady on the left is holding a Bible and note the kettle hanging over a camp fire on the extreme right.

LOOKING EAST DOWN MILL LANE. The sale yard is to the left of the photographer and the horse with no bridle or saddle is about to be sold or has just been bought.

THE SCHOOL. This site was originally owned by the Calthorpe family and on it stood a tithe barn, the roof timbers of which were incorporated in the school. On the right is the shop of Mr Rix the Harness Maker. A hand-stitched leather handbag made by him is still in the possession of Mr Trevor Bradford.

ACLE RUN circa 1878. This dyke was the main drain for land south of the village and was probably a river or stream 1500 years ago. As the name implies water was continually running along the dyke and a pond existed along its course where Fred Colk's wood yard now is.

RAILWAY WORKS 1880. The drainage pipes shown were used in large numbers and as with the By-pass many problems occurred especially in the area between Reedham Road and Spring Dyke. I am told that the Great Eastern Railway Company solved their problems by pushing old railway trucks on top of each other into the boggy marsh and created the embankment on top. This photograph was taken looking south, to the left is at present Howlett and Edrich Sale Yard and the station on the far right.

VIEW DOWN DAMGATE LANE BEFORE THE TURN OF THE CENTURY.
The King Billy pub is on the extreme left.

VIEW OF THE CHAPEL AND MIDDLESEX TERRACE. The By-pass now runs through here.

THE 20th CENTURY

Queen Victoria died in 1901. As a result of easier working conditions and new attitudes to leisure, an industry was being born that was to change Acle throughout the century — the tourist industry.

The Enclosures Acts in the 18th Century had allowed the construction of boat dykes and staithes and goods were delivered by boats and wherries close to the villages.

Local people used these areas for recreation and sailing was becoming more popular. In 1890 the first Acle Regatta was held with 150 yachts taking part. By 1908 Blakes were hiring sailing cruisers and the Broads holiday had arrived. Boat yards were to be built on Boat Dyke and at Acle Bridge bringing employment and prosperity to the region. Acle came to be known as the Gateway to the Broads.

1909 was the year the Old Age Pension was introduced and Henry Ford started a production line for the Model T Ford. In 1912 floods created havoc pushing along the railway line from Brundall to Acle; the marshes were under water again. The Titanic sank the same year. A Dutch family, Van Rossum, built the first sugar beet factory at Cantley and soon many men from Acle were employed there.

Great Britain declared war on Germany on August 4th 1914. On April 25th 1916 German warships bombarded Great Yarmouth and hundreds of people evacuated the town, taking refuge at the Acle New Road. The town looked a little different then. The area where Waters Sale Yard now exists was called Hall Close and in those days village sports were held there and once a travelling circus put on a performance. What is today Lloyds Bank was then two cottages-one used as a gentlemen's outfitters. It was owned by a tailor who set up as a barber at weekends. He was known as *"Bishybarnybee"* and was a beloved Acle character. Peace was declared in 1919 with a Union Jack flown from the top of the Folly Tree. Two years later Acle War Memorial was unveiled by Edward Cushion and Owen Waters, both of whom had lost their fathers fighting in France. The memorial near the church commemorates 28 dead from Acle.

On the 16th December 1919, Howlett and Edrich held their first Sale opposite the church. The owners of the small piece of land on the corner of Reedham Road built a cafe here realising the potential it would have. It wasn't until many years later that Howlett and Edrich bought the cafe and used it for their office.

1920 saw the establishment of Acle St. Edmunds Bowls Club which played on the Rectory lawn. Members were known as the *"Holy Boys".* The Acle Show was an annual event at this time held either on the Rectory lawn or on a marsh in Damgate. The show consisted of maypole dancing, tug-of-war, pillow fighting and a baby show. At the entrance to the Yarmouth Old Road a small building had been added to the Manor house and used as a butcher's shop by Jack Hodds and Elsie Bond. During the war it had been used as a gun emplacement but sadness spread over Acle when Jimmy Griffin, a painter and decorator, was found to have hanged himself inside the building.

The toll payment to travel along the Acle New Road was abolished in 1921 and scores of tramps passed through the village from Lingwood workhouse and slept in a hedge on the Norwich Road which soon came to be known as *"Tramps' hedge"*.

Acle United Football Club was formed in 1913 and in 1923 they played in the final of the Wiltshire Cup. They beat Southtown United 4-2 and it was the first time the cup had left the Borough of Great Yarmouth. The team was supported by nearly all the village with a *"Football Special"* train running from Acle to Great Yarmouth. The players were used to good support with over a thousand turning up to watch important matches.

The famous *"John Knowlittle"* gave a lecture in Acle in November 1924 and told of a Black Tern nesting at Upton and stories concerning the local poachers, *"Cadge"* Brown and *"Shortun"* Page.

1927 saw the start of a sixty-two year battle when the people of Acle proposed that a by-pass be built. Doctor Day moved to Acle in 1927 and was in practice until 1935. Dr Day went on to write a book using the pseudonym of Peter Quince entitled The Left Handed Doctor. The book has autobiographical elements and tells of Freethorpe, Halvergate, Reedham and Accliegh and describes many local people and events.

Acle Tennis Club played on hard courts in Mill Lane while local cricket was being dominated by the village of Upton.

There was a clockwork tidal gauge at Acle Bridge in 1930 which measured the rise and fall of the tide. In 1931 the three-arch bridge was replaced by the current one.

The East and West Flegg District Council amalgamated with Blofield and District Council in 1930 and in 1932 the Acle Labour Exchange was a well supported venue. Friday was pay day and a continuous queue formed all day at the door of the wooden hut. Unemployment was a result not only of the Depression but also of the continuing changes in agricultural practices; the days of the horse were numbered and horse power was being measured with tractors in mind. The coming of the tractor changed the countryside as farmers turned small fields into large plains. Banks and hedgerows were removed by the hundreds affecting the habits of birds, animals and humans.

GEORGE THOMPSON STANDING IN FRONT OF HIS GARAGE circa 1930. The garage stood opposite the Cottage Restaurant on the Old Road in Acle. Not the petrol pumps were hand cranked and believed to be the first to be installed in Norfolk. George was a cabinet maker by trade and had worked on making aircraft for Boulton and Paul in Norwich. He had a high reputation as a meticulous craftsman and a grandfather clock built by him still keeps perfect time in Mr Dudley Blake's bungalow today.

1935 brought Dr Fletcher to practise in Acle and he lived in Robin Hall until 1937 when he moved to the White House on the South Walsham Road. The police moved from Reedham Road station to a new building on the Norwich Road in 1938.

The Nazis invaded Poland on September 1st 1939 and Britain entered the war two days later. Acle was declared a strategic spot in the event of an invasion. This had happened before-during the Napoleonic wars it had been planned that Acle bridge would be blown up and every man in the area would converge on Acle to fight the enemy under the leadership of Brigadier General Lord Orford. Times had changed but not the strategy; so once more Acle Bridge was mined in case the Germans landed. Pill boxes were built around the village and gun emplacements as well as searchlights were soon to become commonplace. The first bombs to fell on Norfolk on May 25th 1940. Acle people continued to live as normally as possible-advertisements in the deanery magazine included Sewell's Bakery for Norfolk Hollow Biscuits, Sydney Jeary for home-killed meats, and George Thompson for wireless sets. Nevertheless the most frequently bombed places were Caister-on-Sea and Halvergate Marshes.

After the Second World War life changed for everyone. The marshes started to lose their stately windpumps and the new efficiency of the electric pumps undermined the wildlife of the region. The geese population alone was soon drastically reduced.

Clothes rationing ended in March 1949. In January 1953 the legendary floods devastated the area as they did so much of the Norfolk coast.

Acle expanded rapidly and became the mother village for its surrounding neighbours largely because of its two markets and the flower and vegetable auctions. It was an ideal place for local people to sell their produce to the hotel trade in Yarmouth.

Traffic increased steadily and in 1955 Mr Clarence White was appointed as the school's Lollipop man. The following year saw the establishment of a Roman Catholic Chapel where the first Roman Mass was celebrated for 400 years.

The Tacolneston transmitter opened in 1955 bringing television to the area and in 1957 Russia launched the first satellite.

Acle Secondary Modern School opened in 1959 and plans were made to widen the Acle Straight into a dual carriageway. In March 1963 the Yarmouth Co-Operative took over Rix's — Acle's most famous store for nearly a century. A yacht marina was proposed for Acle as the Swinging Sixties got under way.

Gas was discovered off Great Yarmouth. In 1968 the King William IV public house on Damgate closed. Affectionately known as the King Billy, it attracted many unusual characters and particularly fishermen wanting a good night out. The beer was contained in pails set around the floor and old games such as ringing the hook on the wall with a ring suspended from the ceiling were very popular. Some of its regulars walked across the marshes from Tunstall. But pop music was the coming thing and a local group called *"Exhibit A"* performed on Saturday nights at the Stracey Arms.

The Broadland Study and Plan was published in 1971 reporting 12,000 cars a day using the Acle Straight and announcing a study into the possibility of a Bure-Yare cut. This would allow river traffic to pass between rivers without entering Great Yarmouth.

Sewells Bakery closed in 1972 and a new bridge into Yarmouth from the Acle Straight was opened. Acle village sign was unveiled in 1974 and in the same year Howlett and Edrich held the first horse sale in the village for 25 years. A mare and foal fetched 320 and a Tinker's cart made 260. *"Herondale"*, a short stay home for the elderly and the second of its kind in the country, opened in 1975. 1976 saw the opening of Acle Health Centre by Sir Arthur South.

Mr Malcom Porter found himself in a dilemma in 1977 as to what to do with the cafe the *"Singing Kettle"* which had received a mention in the Egon Ronay Guide. The cafe was an 1890 six-wheeled Great Eastern railway carriage. It had been bought by Mr William Coman for 20 in 1928 and been on the site ever since, but now the land was needed for building. Mr Porter was reluctant to dismantle it and offered it to anyone who would restore it. Eventually it was transported to Sheringham for the North Norfolk Railway and is still used today as a carpenter's workshop.

"Palmers Post Mill" was a erected at Upton by Mr Michael Seago and restored to its former glory. The mill had pumped from marshland on the New Road at Acle before becoming obsolete; the site today is to become a Little Chef Motel.

In June 1977 the Queen's Jubilee was celebrated in Acle with a carnival and the opening of a New Recreation Centre for the village. In torrential rain much fun was had by all and the Norwich City Football Manager, John Bond, opened the new Centre which in a few years became one of the best in Norfolk.

In 1979 Acle lost one of its most famous landmarks, the folly tree; it was lopped because of Dutch Elm Disease and its dangerous position near the main road.

ACLE GREEN AND FOLLY TREE. The Folly Tree dominates the village street and was certainly in existence in 1815 when it was mentioned by Edmund Harrison. It may have been given its name because it was foolish to plant a tree so close to the main road and on a bend. Or it may have been planted on the site of a previous building known as a folly.

In the summer of the same year residents in the area relived some of the anxiety of the Second World War when twelve 500lb bombs were discovered in the buried wreckage of an American Liberator bomber which had crashed near Acle in 1944. The bombs were exploded in a specially dug pit on the marshes and during the controlled explosions the railway line and the Acle Straight were closed.

The last ten years have seen few major changes in Acle although the building of a new primary school and the sale the old school for £510,000 was, and will be, of significance.

However, the most recent change is also the biggest change in the last hundred years. The By-pass will create a new environment which will either bring wealth or turn the village into a dormitory for Great Yarmouth and Norwich. The responsibility for Acle's future depends on District and Parish Council's control, and most importantly on the parishioners themselves. Development and the maintaining of a market will help but the provision of public services must be maintained. Environmental issues will certainly make headlines and Acle, on the edge of the most important wetlands, in Britain must be allowed its say.

There is one other item of interest that should be recorded as part of the 20th Century. For some reason Acle suffers hardly any vandalism or teenage hooliganism-instead the youngsters involve themselves with the community. I have not discovered Acle's secret formula but it is a fact, and Acle's teenagers are proud of it. Let's hope it won't change. I have asked one old resident of Acle how he saw the future and he said, *"Well blast me boy, unless things change, they'll remain the same."*

KINGS HEAD AND OLD FOLLY TREE. *This photograph was obviously posed for by all-including the lady leaning out of the King's head window.*